Things I Say to Me

Jibril Collins

Presentation by *BookLeaf Publishing*

Web: www.bookleafpub.com

E-mail: info@bookleafpub.com

ISBN: 9789358367720

First edition 2023

I dedicate this book to nature.

Peace and Love

Morning Dew

1

Participate in the day
for that's where the secrets lay

Songbird

Dear songbird I wonder
In the darkest of light
Silence of sound
Intrinsic to imagination
Permeate reality
One is it's own
until it loves

Leafs

3

Hold on,
to what you hold on to
stuck are the wet leaves
the one dry leaf, blows
as long as the wind
 shall breeze.

Things

Do not let "more"
be the thing you want.

Divine

5

Love
is such a divine true,
but
more in hell do it.

Rights

Some words
the dictionary does not
have the right to explain

Luck

7

Luck is karma
with out participation

Stay

Where did all the love go
Where does love stay
Why did it come here
Why'd it go and which way
Where did all the love go
When does it stay
Welcomed for your thank you
I thank you, for your stay
&
I'll stay because, I love you
I'll stay because I'll wait
I'll wait because I love you
I'll wait, so I'll stay

At Lunch

9

Never take
arbitrary
out for lunch

Xoxo's (Hugs & Kisses)

Stars dance
the sun smile's
night blanket
the blue sky

Scared Planet

There is infinite real estate
in the land of what if

All

12

Only the divine
live
in stopped time

Entirely Up to You

13

Beautiful
or new
the rest
is up
to you

Drink

Drink myrrh
produce dew
enjoy serpent
consume the egg
create the stone
consummate
salience bleeds
 up the ladder

Hello Goodbye

15

Strange faces
become familiar
perfect time
wrong place

Dandelion's Child

Some get stomped
Some get found
Some are stuck
Still in the ground
Some are broken
Some get pulled
Some are dead
Still
In your room
None get kept
All are wild
Ancestors of smile
Dandelions Child

Around & Around

17

Around and around
Runs the day,
More is done,
Sitting in the play

Still Morning

Still morning
Storm just passed
The calm deafening
No one in sight
Chirp lost bird
A crow
Makes its way
But that's what crows do
Soaked soil, rubber trees
The planet drinks the rain
Heaven this must be
No squalor just trees
Puddles the mind and me

Take "Your Time"

19

Dear Life
my advice
live slow

Silk Sliver

Silk scarf
Silk road
Silver lining
Madness Twinkle
Reality dances
with you my friend

Somethings have no name

21

Letters
cry
when
written
down

www.ingramcontent.com/pod-product-compliance
Lightning Source LLC
LaVergne TN
LVHW051252200726
843510LV00011B/1815